EASY PIANO

The Barney SONGBOOK ™

ISBN 0-634-02825-1

HAL•LEONARD®
CORPORATION

7777 W. BLUEMOUND RD. P.O. BOX 13819 MILWAUKEE, WI 53213

© 2001 Lyons Partnership, L.P.
All Rights Reserved

The Barney and BJ names and characters and the overlapping dino spots and Barney and star logos
are trademarks of Lyons Partnership, L.P. Reg. U.S. Pat. and Tm. Office.
The Baby Bop name and character, Super-Dee-Duper and BJ and the Rockets are trademarks of Lyons Partnership, L.P.

For all works contained herein:
Unauthorized copying, arranging, adapting, recording or public performance is an infringement of copyright.
Infringers are liable under the law.

Visit Hal Leonard Online at
www.halleonard.com

BARNEY THEME SONG

Traditional Music ("Yankee Doodle")
Lyrics by STEPHEN BATES BALTES
and PHILIP A. PARKER

Copyright © 1990, 1992 Shimbaree Music (ASCAP)
All Rights Reserved   Used by Permission

Bar - ney's friends are big and small; they come from lots of plac - es:

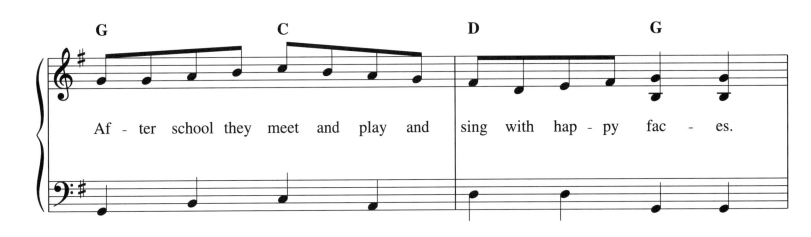

Af - ter school they meet and play and sing with hap - py fac - es.

Bar - ney shows us lots of things like how to play pre - tend, _____

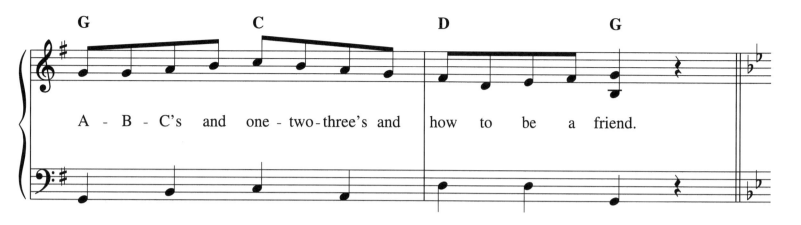

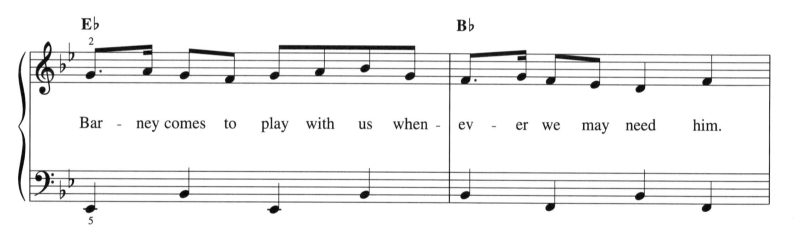

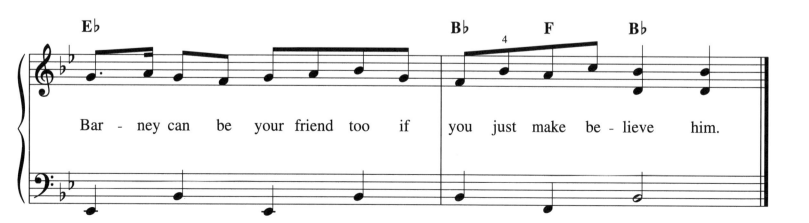

ALPHABET SONG

Traditional

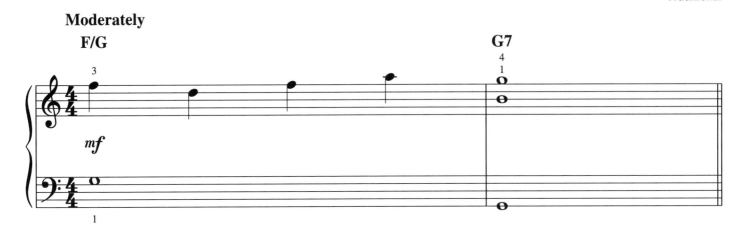

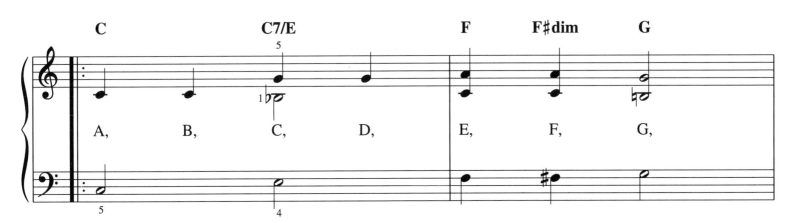

A,   B,   C,   D,   E,   F,   G,

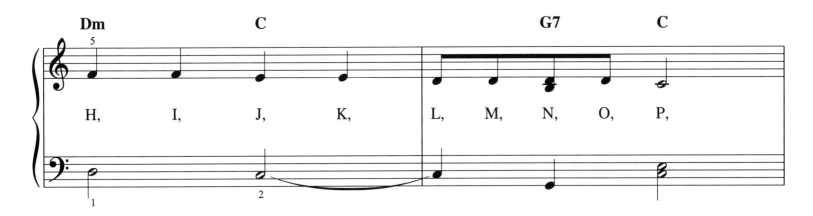

H,   I,   J,   K,   L,   M,   N,   O,   P,

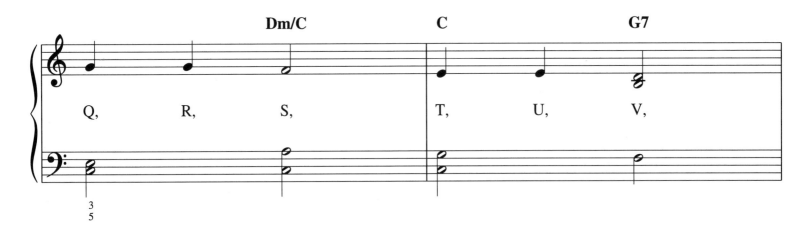

Q,   R,   S,   T,   U,   V,

Arrangement Copyright © 1992 Shimbarah Music (BMI)
A Division of Lyons Partnership, L.P.
All Rights Reserved   Used by Permission

THE BABY BOP HOP

Music and Lyrics by STEPHEN BATES BALTES
and LORY LAZARUS

Copyright © 1995 Shimbaree Music (ASCAP)
A Division of Lyons Partnership, L.P.
All Rights Reserved   Used by Permission

Dm   Dm/C   G7   C

"Ba - by Bop, do the Ba - by Bop Hop." Hop! Hop! Hop!

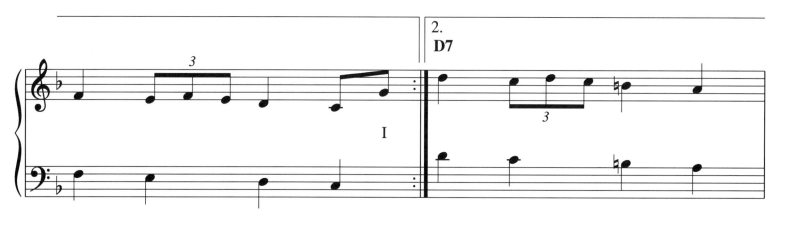

Hop!   Hop!   Hop!   Hop!

1.

2.
D7

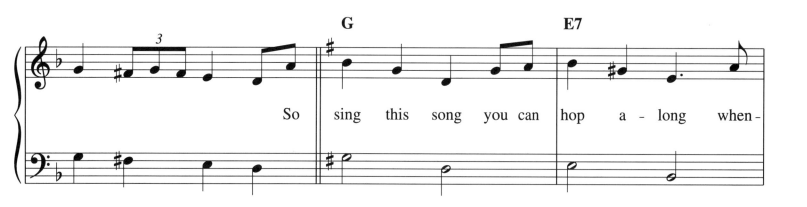

G   E7

So sing this song you can hop a - long when-

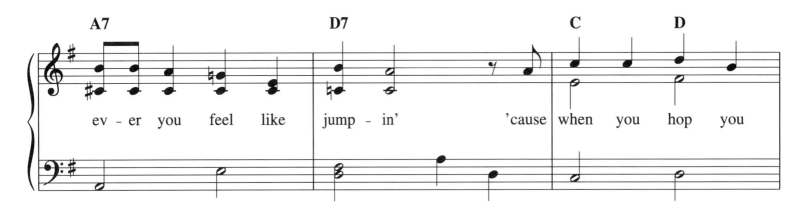

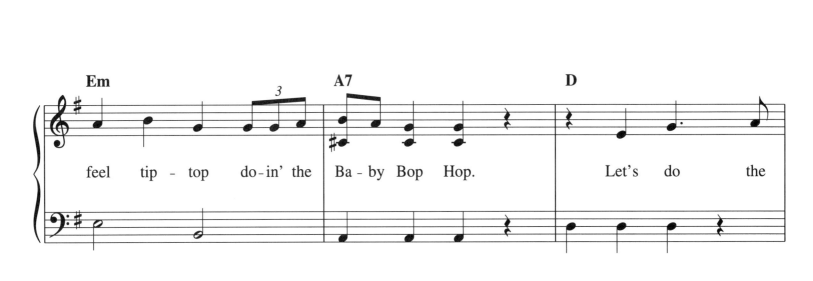

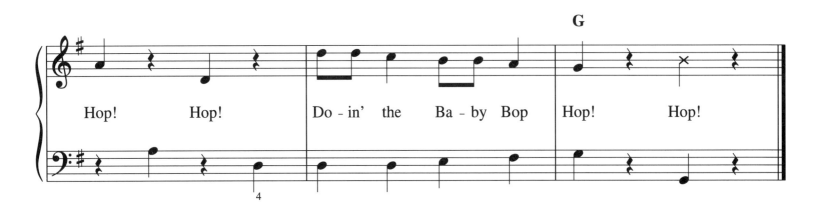

AND THE GREEN GRASS
GROWS ALL AROUND

Traditional

Moderately

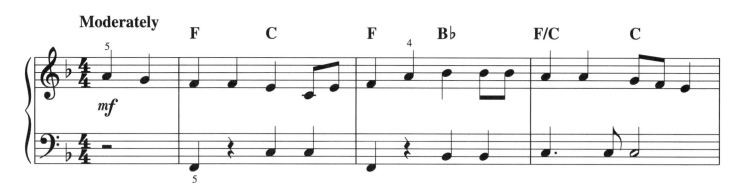

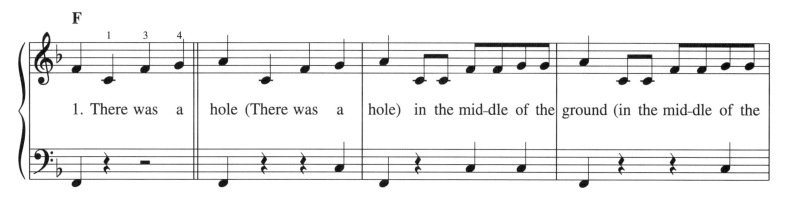

1. There was a hole (There was a hole) in the mid-dle of the ground (in the mid-dle of the

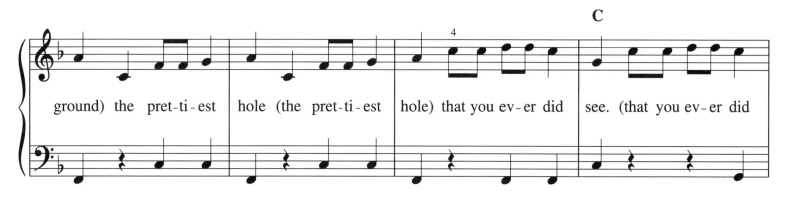

ground) the pret-ti-est hole (the pret-ti-est hole) that you ev-er did see. (that you ev-er did

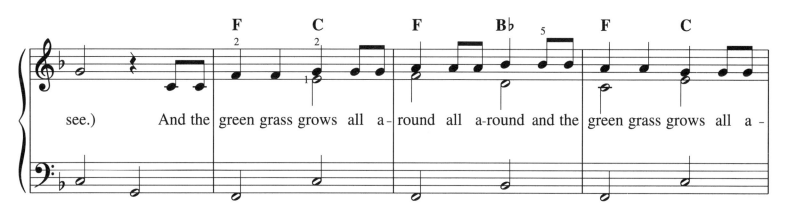

see.) And the green grass grows all a-round all a-round and the green grass grows all a-

Arrangement Copyright © 1992 Shimbarah Music (BMI)
A Division of Lyons Partnership, L.P.
All Rights Reserved   Used by Permission

Additional Lyrics

NOTE: *Each verse adds an item which is then added to the list at the front of the chorus. The final chorus is on the next page.*

3. And on this tree   (Echo)
   There was a branch   (Echo)
   The prettiest branch   (Echo)
   That you ever did see.   (Echo)
   Well, the branch on the tree and the tree in the hole and the hole in the ground and the green grass...
4. And on this branch   (Echo)   there was a nest...
5. And in this nest   (Echo)   there was an egg...
6. And in this egg   (Echo)   there was a bird...

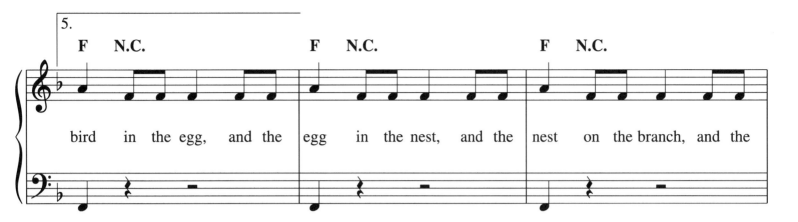

bird in the egg, and the egg in the nest, and the nest on the branch, and the

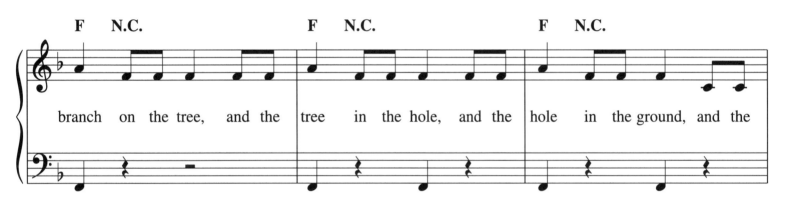

branch on the tree, and the tree in the hole, and the hole in the ground, and the

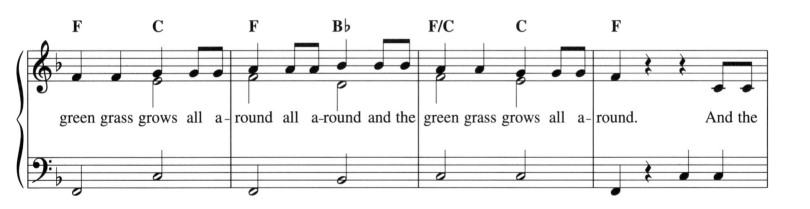

green grass grows all a-round all a-round and the green grass grows all a-round. And the

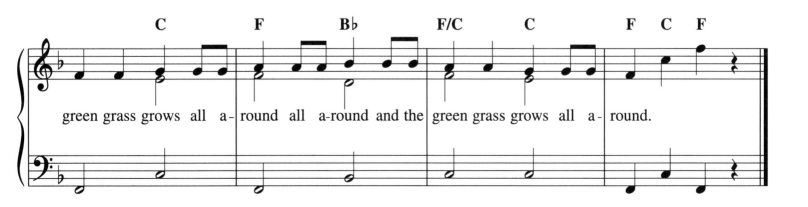

green grass grows all a-round all a-round and the green grass grows all a-round.

BINGO

Traditional

Moderately fast

1. There was a farm-er had a dog and
3.-6. *(See additional lyrics)*

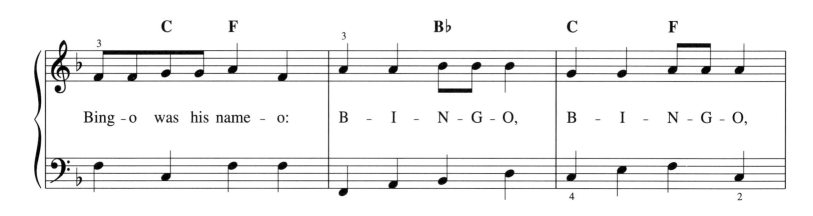

Bing-o was his name-o: B - I - N - G - O, B - I - N - G - O,

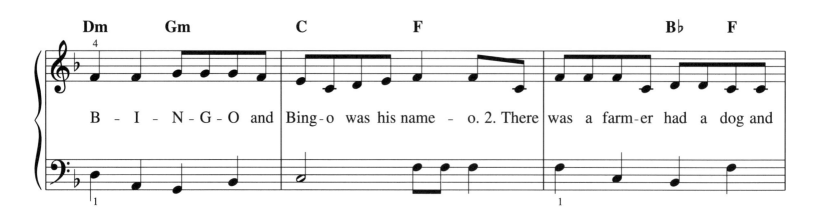

B - I - N - G-O and Bing-o was his name - o. 2. There was a farm-er had a dog and

Arrangement Copyright © 1992 Shimbarah Music (BMI)
A Division of Lyons Partnership, L.P.
All Rights Reserved   Used by Permission

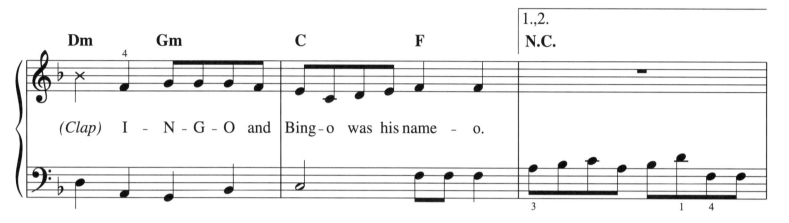

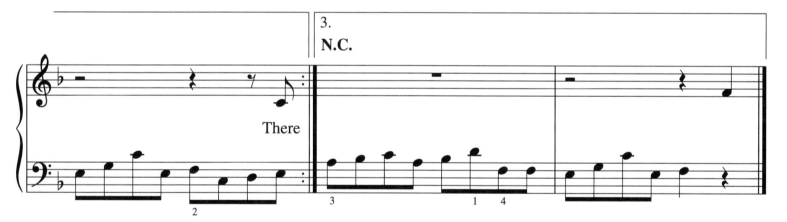

Additional Lyrics

3. There was a farmer had a dog and Bingo was his name-o:
- - N-G-O, - - N-G-O, - - N-G-O
And Bingo was his name-o.

4. There was a farmer had a dog and Bingo was his name-o:
- - - G-O, - - - G-O, - - - G-O
And Bingo was his name-o.

5. There was a farmer had a dog and Bingo was his name-o:
- - - - O, - - - - O, - - - - O
And Bingo was his name-o.

6. There was a farmer had a dog and Bingo was his name-o:
- - - - -, - - - - -, - - - - -
And Bingo was his name-o.

BOOM, BOOM, AIN'T IT GREAT TO BE CRAZY?

Traditional

Moderately, with a swing feel

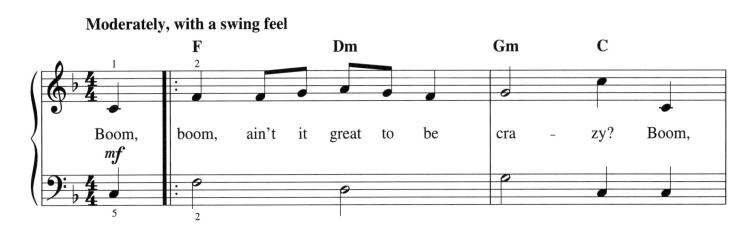

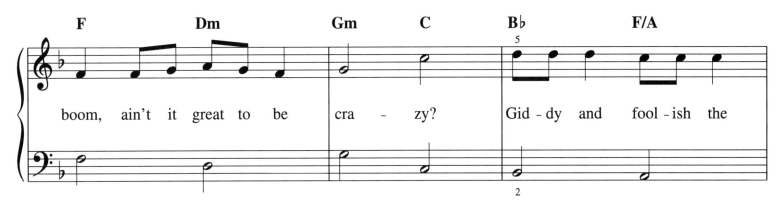

Arrangement Copyright © 1992 Shimbarah Music (BMI)
A Division of Lyons Partnership, L.P.
All Rights Reserved   Used by Permission

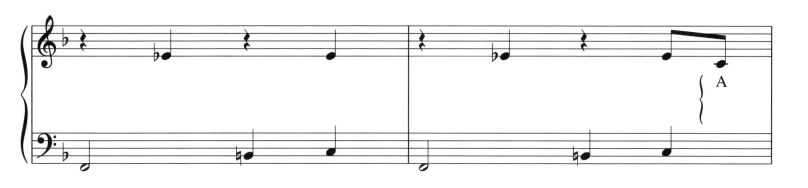

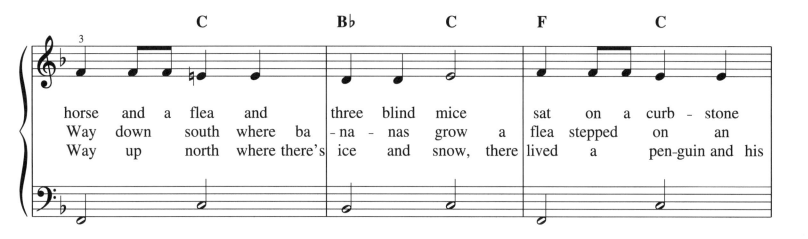

horse and a flea and | three blind mice | sat on a curb - stone
Way down south where ba -na - nas grow a | flea stepped on an
Way up north where there's ice and snow, there | lived a pen-guin and his

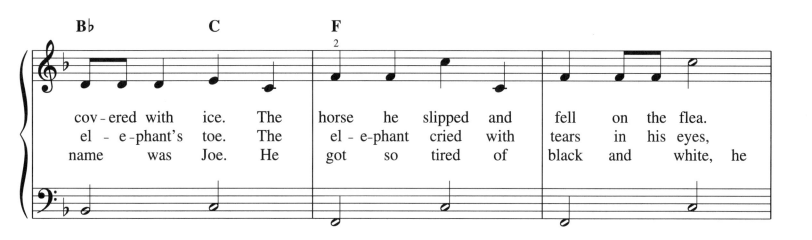

cov - ered with ice. The | horse he slipped and | fell on the flea.
el - e -phant's toe. The | el - e-phant cried with | tears in his eyes,
name was Joe. He | got so tired of | black and white, he

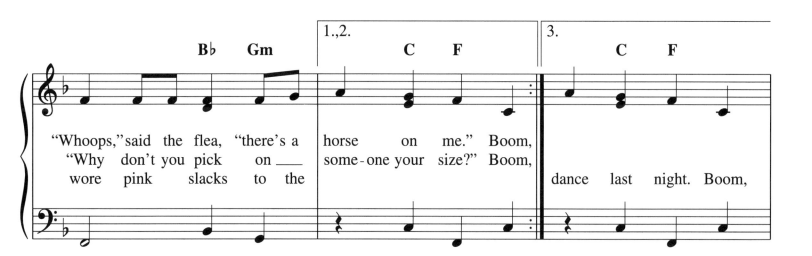

"Whoops," said the flea, "there's a | horse on me." Boom,
"Why don't you pick on ___ | some-one your size?" Boom,
wore pink slacks to the | dance last night. Boom,

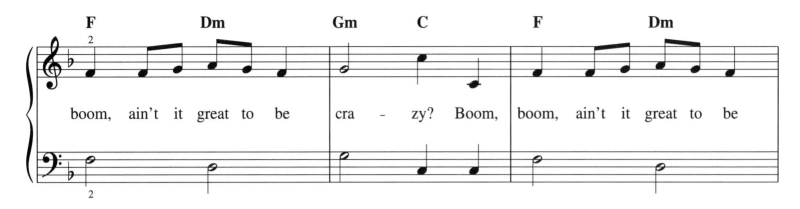

boom, ain't it great to be cra - zy? Boom, boom, ain't it great to be

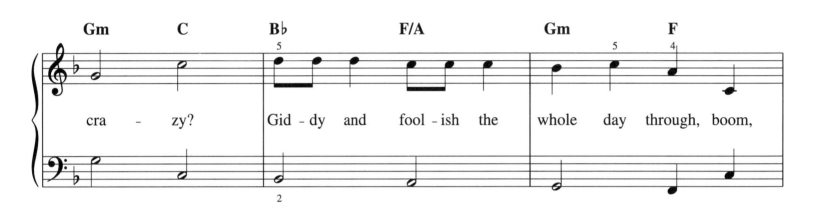

cra - zy? Gid - dy and fool - ish the whole day through, boom,

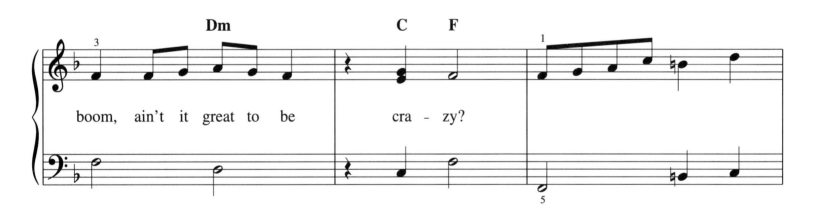

boom, ain't it great to be cra - zy?

Cra - zy!

CLEAN UP

Traditional

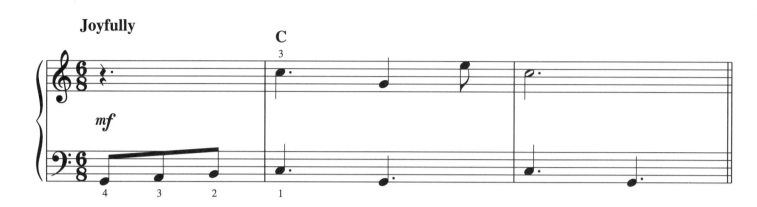

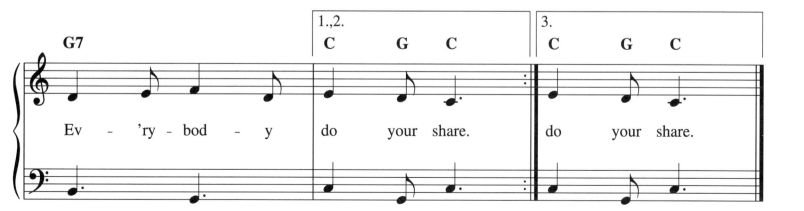

Arrangement Copyright © 1992 Shimbarah Music (BMI)
A Division of Lyons Partnership, L.P.
All Rights Reserved   Used by Permission

BUMPIN' UP AND DOWN

Traditional

Bump-in' up and down in my lit-tle red wag-on,
March-in' all a-round in my lit-tle red wag-on,

bump-in' up and down in my lit-tle red wag-on,
march-in' all a-round in my lit-tle red wag-on,

bump-in' up and down in my
march-in' all a-round in my

lit-tle red wag-on.}
lit-tle red wag-on.}

Won't you be my dar-lin'?

dar-lin'?

Arrangement Copyright © 1993 Shimbarah Music (BMI)
A Division of Lyons Partnership, L.P.
All Rights Reserved   Used by Permission

Roll - in' up and down in my
Bump-in' up and down in my

lit - tle red wag - on,   roll - in' up and down in my   lit - tle red wag - on,
lit - tle red wag - on,   bump-in' up and down in my   lit - tle red wag - on,

roll - in' up and down in my   lit - tle red wag - on.   Won't you be my
bump-in' up and down in my   lit - tle red wag - on.   Won't you be my

1.
dar - lin'?

2.
dar - lin'?   Won't you be my   dar - lin'?

COLORS MAKE ME HAPPY

Music and Lyrics by
WILLY WELCH

Copyright © 1999 Shimbaree Music (ASCAP)
A Division of Lyons Partnership, L.P.
All Rights Reserved   Used by Permission

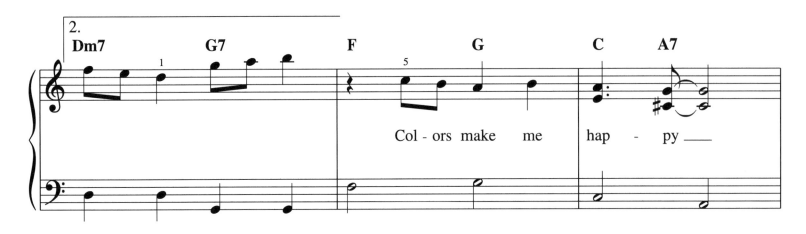

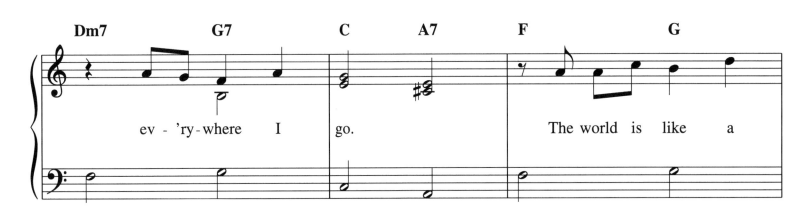

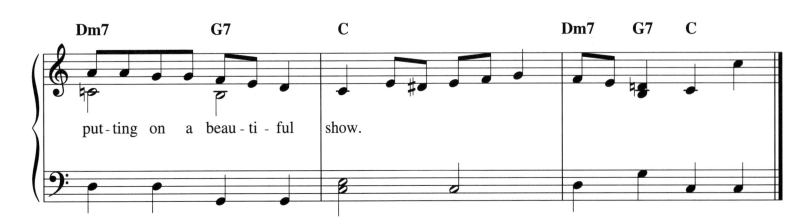

DO YOUR EARS HANG LOW?

Traditional

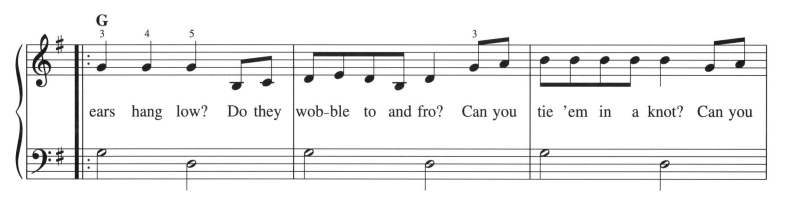

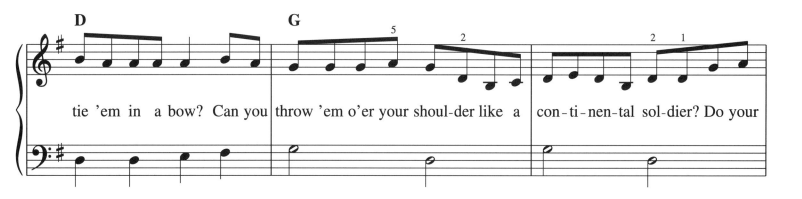

Arrangement Copyright © 1992 Shimbarah Music (BMI)
A Division of Lyons Partnership, L.P.
All Rights Reserved   Used by Permission

DOWN ON GRANDPA'S FARM

Traditional

Moderately fast

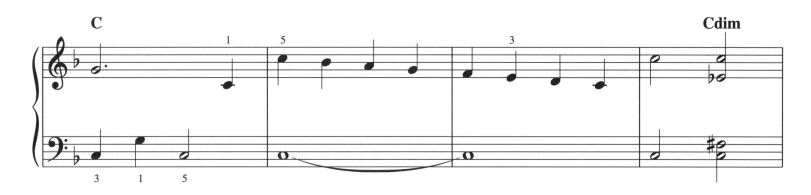

We're on our way, we're on our way, on our

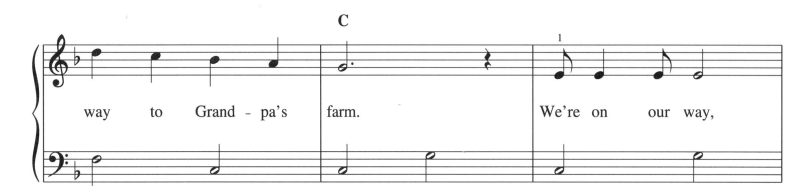

way to Grand-pa's farm. We're on our way,

Arrangement Copyright © 1992 Shimbarah Music (BMI)
A Division of Lyons Partnership, L.P.
All Rights Reserved   Used by Permission

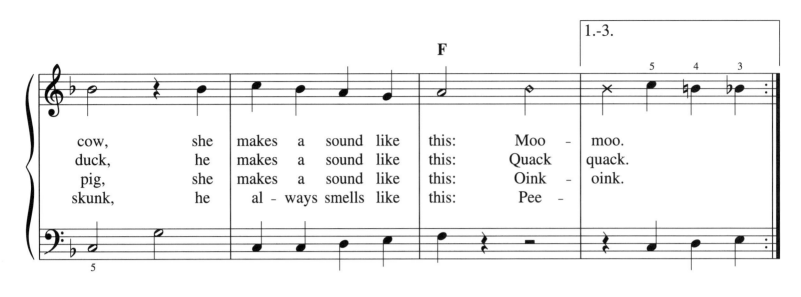

cow,   she   makes   a   sound   like   this: Moo - moo.
duck,   he   makes   a   sound   like   this: Quack   quack.
pig,   she   makes   a   sound   like   this: Oink - oink.
skunk, he   al - ways smells like   this: Pee -

yuu.   We're on   our way,   we're on   our way,   on our

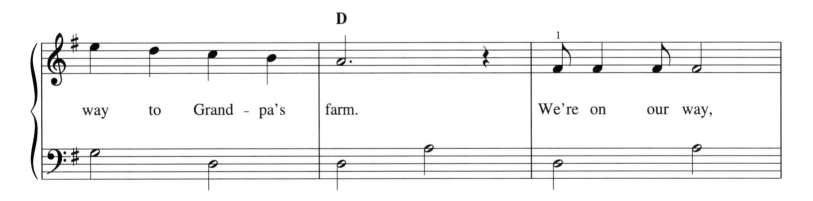

way   to Grand - pa's   farm.   We're on   our way,

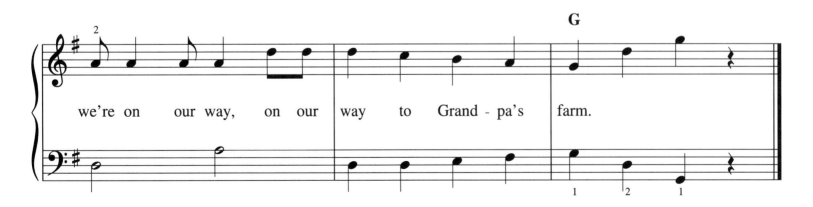

we're on   our way,   on our   way   to   Grand - pa's   farm.

ITSY BITSY SPIDER

Traditional

With a swing feel

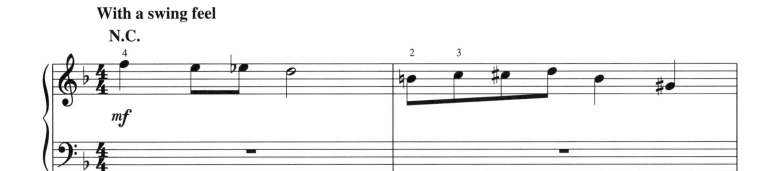

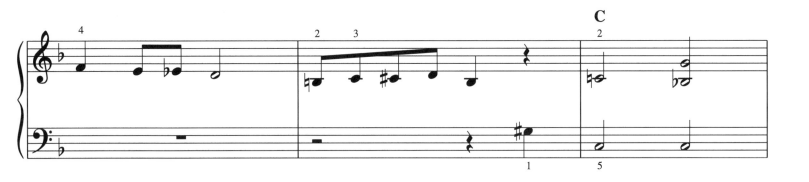

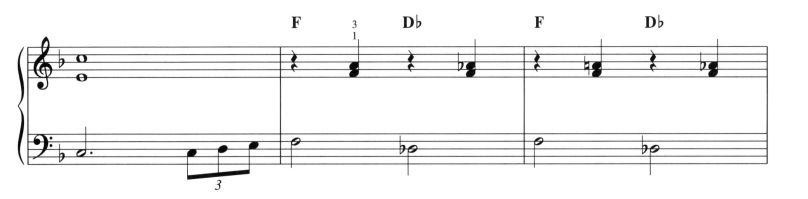

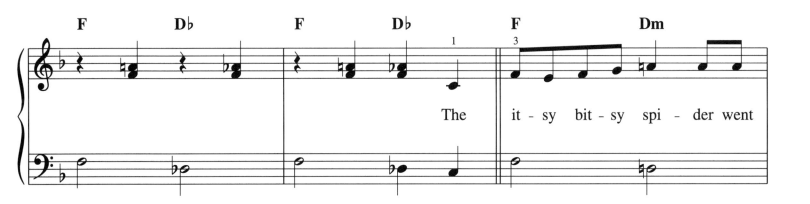

The it-sy bit-sy spi-der went

Arrangement Copyright © 1992 Shimbarah Music (BMI)
A Division of Lyons Partnership, L.P.
All Rights Reserved   Used by Permission

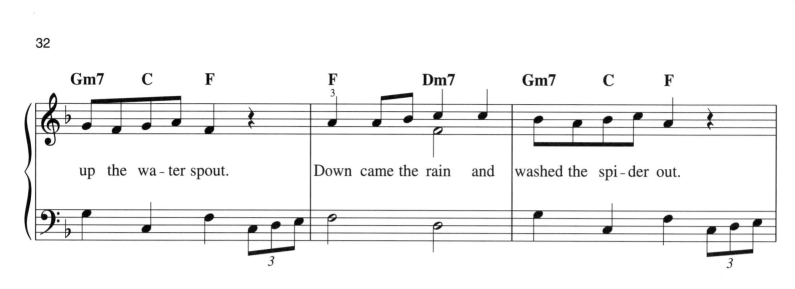

up the wa - ter spout. Down came the rain and washed the spi - der out.

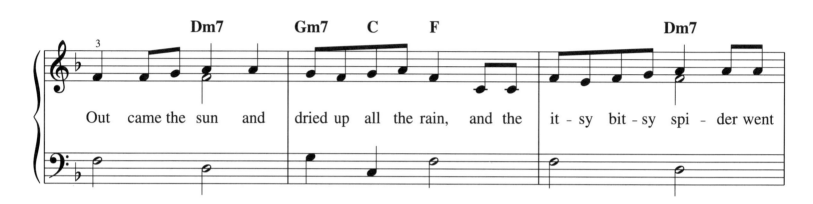

Out came the sun and dried up all the rain, and the it - sy bit - sy spi - der went

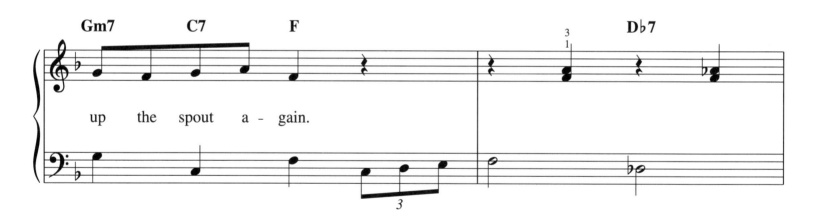

up the spout a - gain.

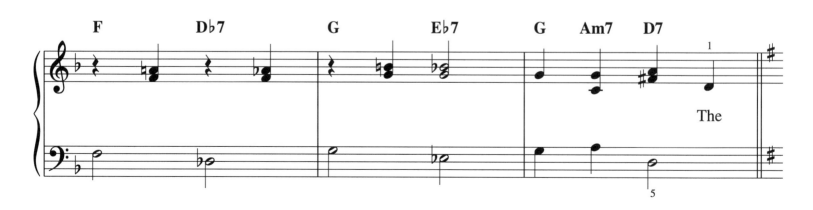

The

it - sy bit - sy spi – der went up the wa - ter spout.

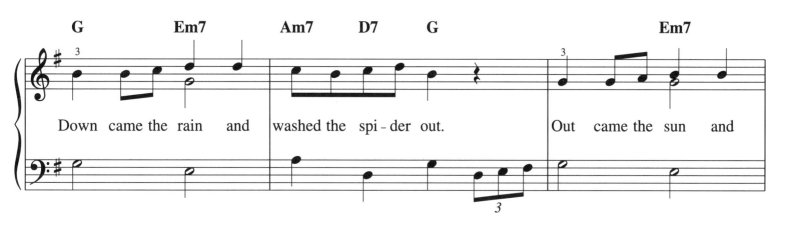

Down came the rain and washed the spi - der out. Out came the sun and

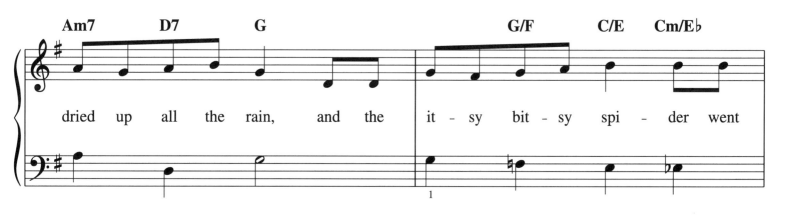

dried up all the rain, and the it - sy bit - sy spi – der went

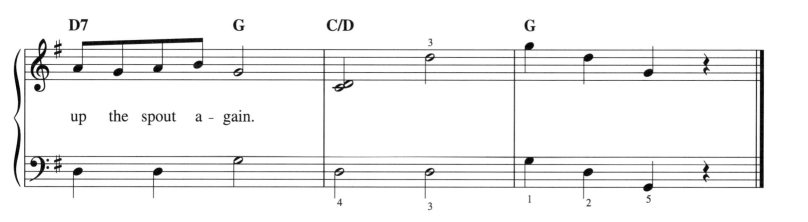

up the spout a - gain.

IF ALL THE RAINDROPS

Traditional

With a swing feel

mf

If

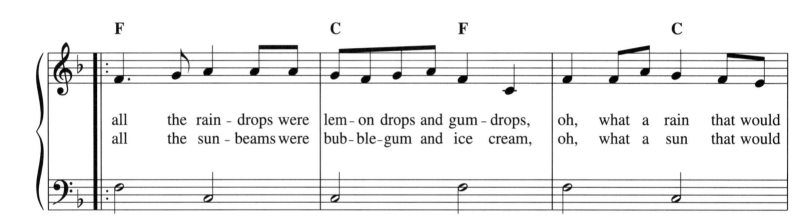

all   the rain - drops were | lem - on drops and gum - drops, | oh,   what a rain   that would
all   the sun - beams were | bub - ble - gum and ice cream, | oh,   what a sun   that would

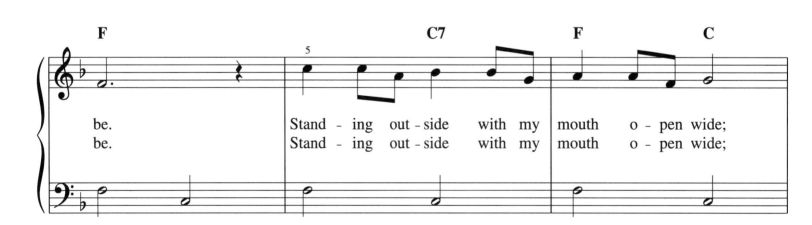

be. | Stand - ing out - side   with my | mouth   o - pen wide;
be. | Stand - ing out - side   with my | mouth   o - pen wide;

Arrangement Copyright © 1992 Shimbarah Music (BMI)
A Division of Lyons Partnership, L.P.
All Rights Reserved   Used by Permission

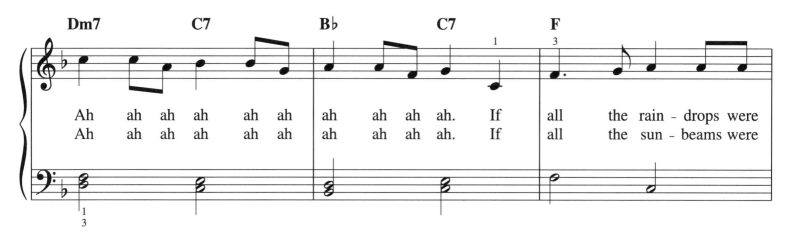

Ah ah ah ah ah ah ah ah ah ah. If all the rain - drops were
Ah ah ah ah ah ah ah ah ah ah. If all the sun - beams were

lem - on drops and gum - drops, oh, what a rain that would
bub – ble – gum and ice cream, oh, what a sun that would

1.

be.

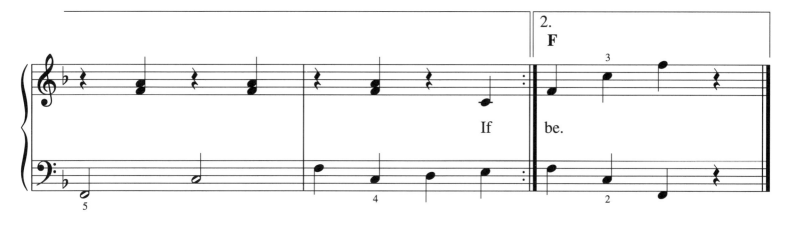

2.

If   be.

THE LAND OF MAKE BELIEVE

Music and Lyrics by
DAVID BERNARD WOLF

Lively, with a swing feel

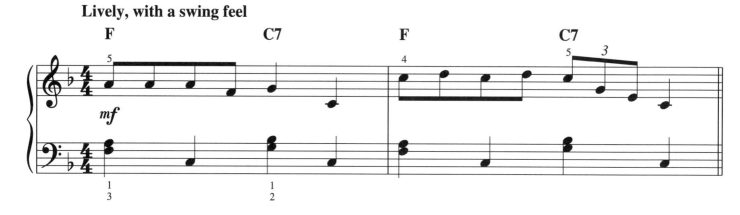

What if lit - tle birds could dance and sing and we could fly with mag - ic wings or
What if we sailed the o - cean in a tub, row - ing while we scrub - a - dub,

may - be for a day I could be King! What if
watch - ing bub - bles fly in - to the sky! What if

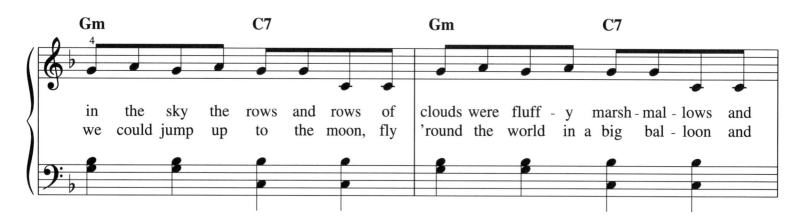

in the sky the rows and rows of clouds were fluff - y marsh - mal - lows and
we could jump up to the moon, fly 'round the world in a big bal - loon and

Copyright © 1996 Super-Dee-Duper Music (SESAC)
A Division of Lyons Partnership, L.P.
All Rights Reserved   Used by Permission

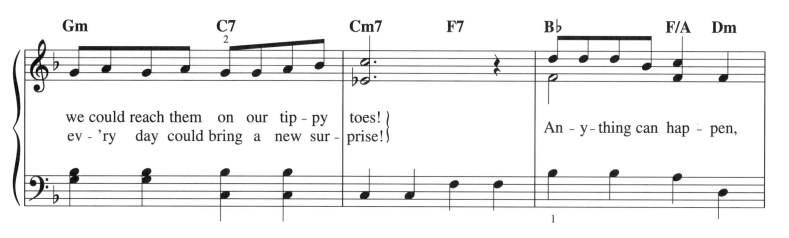

we could reach them on our tip - py toes!
ev - 'ry day could bring a new sur - prise!

An - y - thing can hap - pen,

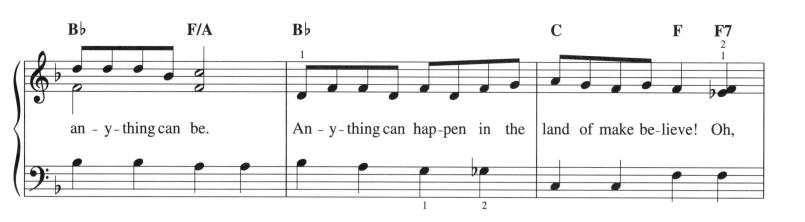

an - y - thing can be. An - y - thing can hap-pen in the land of make be-lieve! Oh,

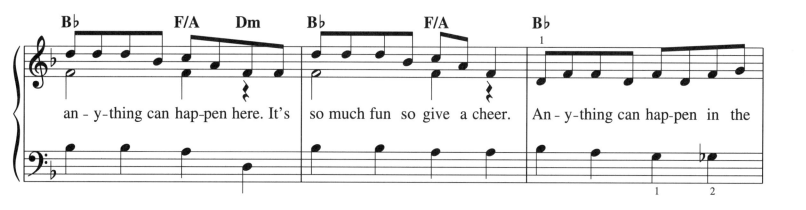

an - y - thing can hap-pen here. It's so much fun so give a cheer. An - y - thing can hap-pen in the

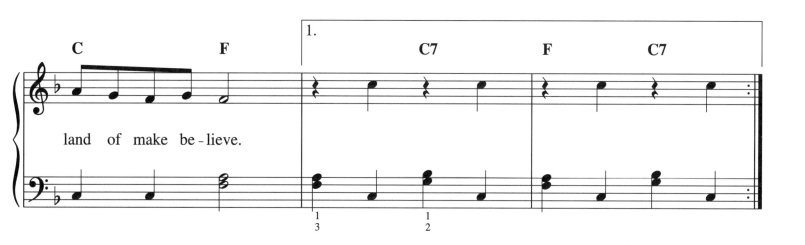

land of make be - lieve.

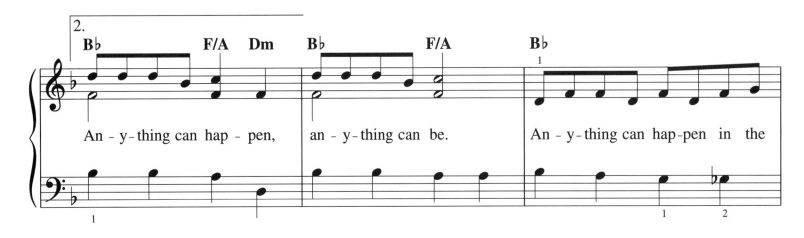

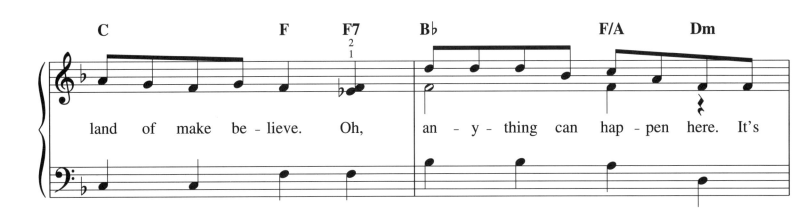

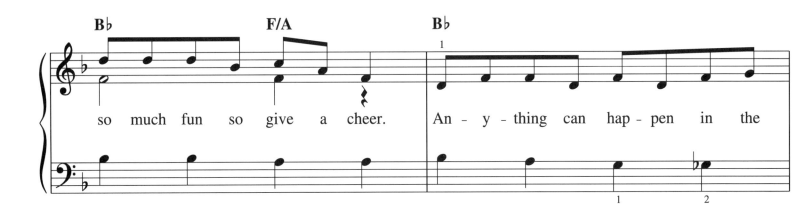

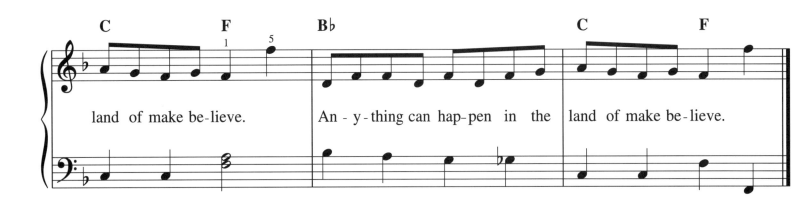

THE NOBLE DUKE OF YORK

Traditional

The no – ble Duke of York, he had ten thou – sand men. He marched them up to the top of the hill and he marched them down a – gain. And

Arrangement Copyright © 1997 Shimbaree Music (ASCAP)
A Division of Lyons Partnership, L.P.
All Rights Reserved   Used by Permission

Am

when you're up, you're up. And when you're down, you're

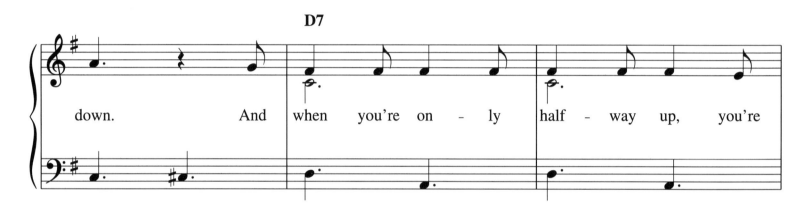

D7

down. And when you're on – ly half – way up, you're

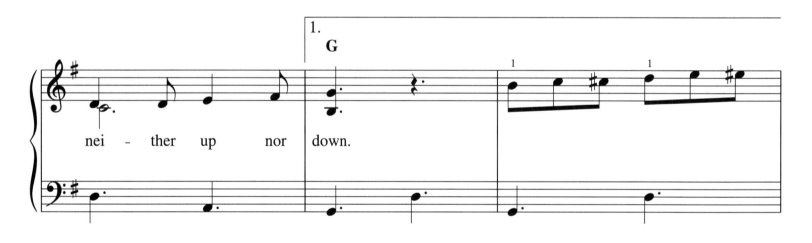

1.

G

nei – ther up nor down.

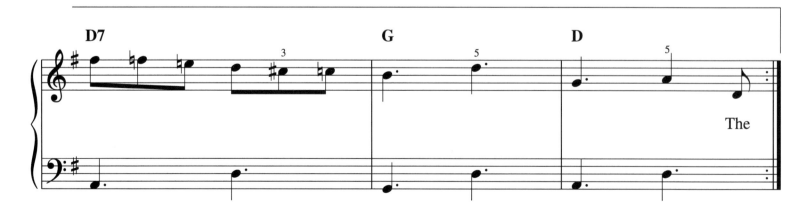

D7   **G**   **D**

The

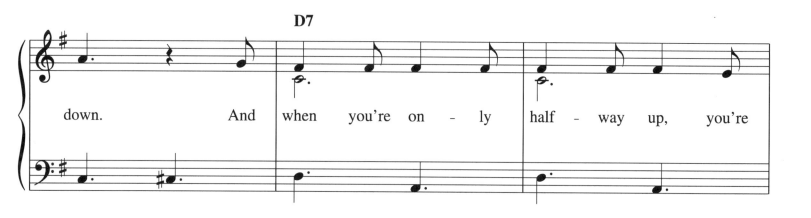

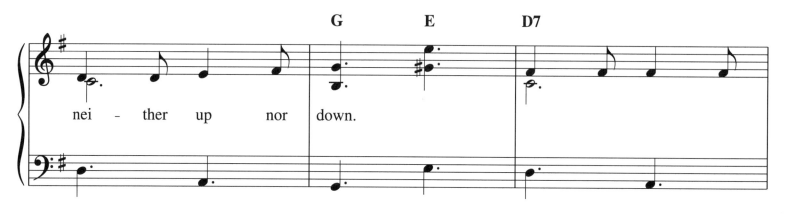

MY FAMILY'S JUST RIGHT FOR ME

Music and Lyrics by
PHILIP A. PARKER

Moderately fast

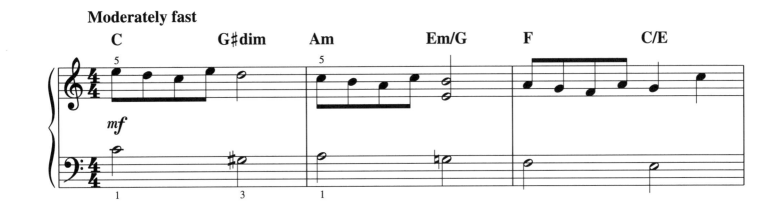

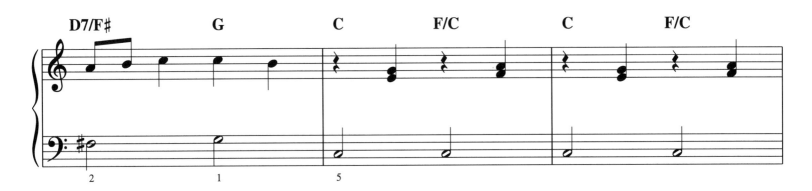

Oh, a fam-i-ly is peo-ple and a

fam-i-ly is love. That's a fam-i-ly. They come in

Copyright © 1992 Shimbaree Music (ASCAP)
A Division of Lyons Partnership, L.P.
All Rights Reserved   Used by Permission

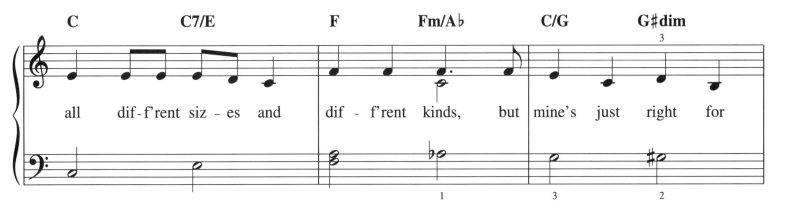

all dif-f'rent siz - es and dif - f'rent kinds, but mine's just right for

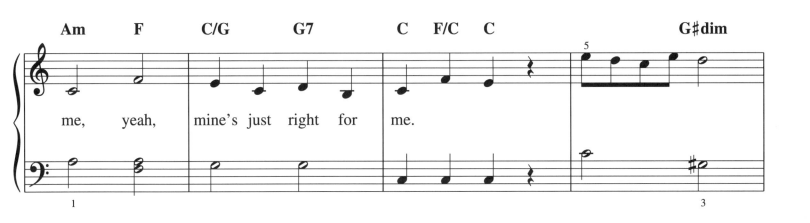

me, yeah, mine's just right for me.

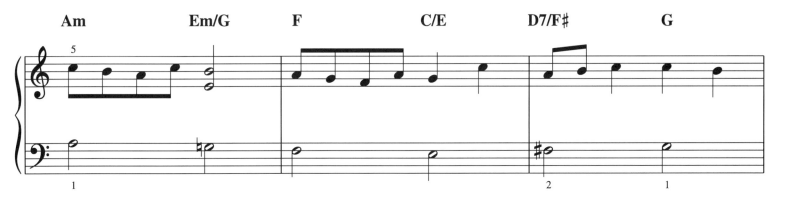

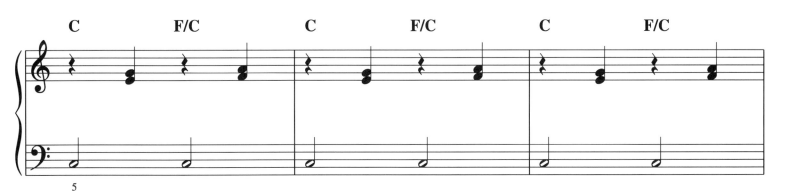

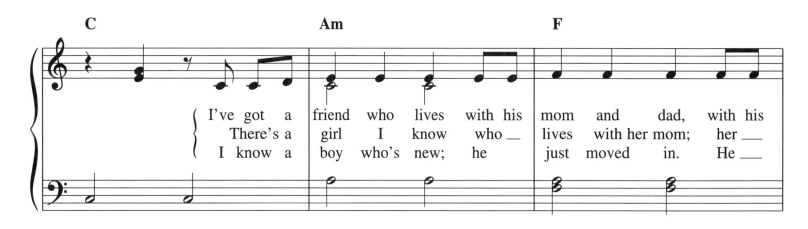

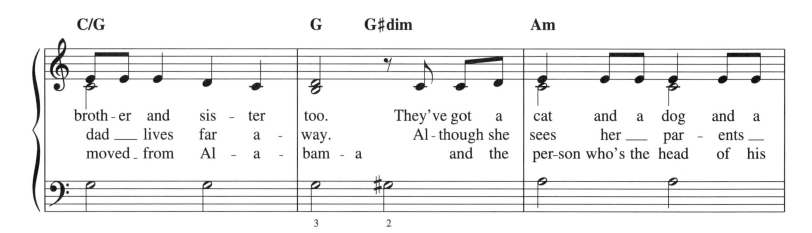

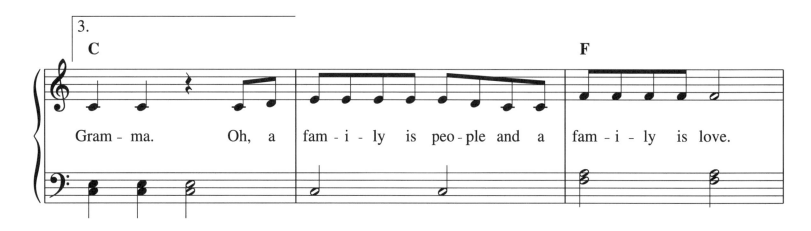

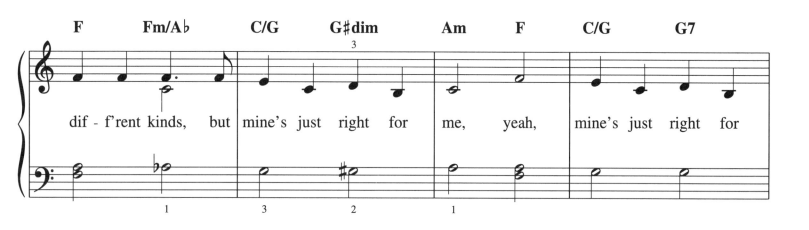

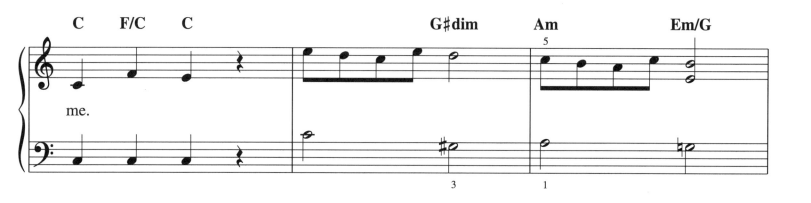

OVER IN THE MEADOW

Traditional

Moderately

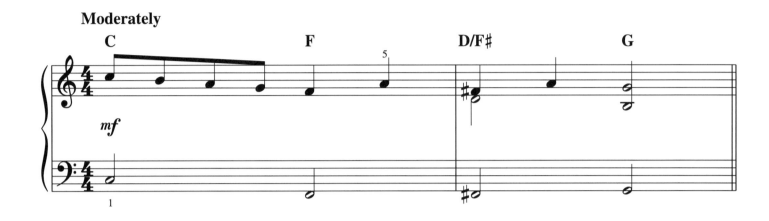

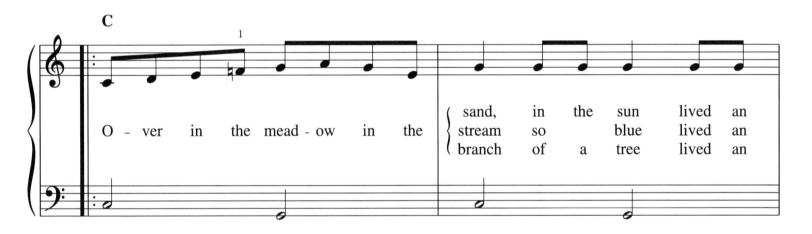

O - ver in the mead - ow in the

sand, in the sun lived an
stream so blue lived an
branch of a tree lived an

old ___ moth - er frog ___ and her lit - tle frog - gie one.
old ___ moth - er fish ___ and her lit - tle fish - ies two.
old ___ moth - er bird ___ and her lit - tle bird - ies three.

Arrangement Copyright © 1992 Shimbarah Music (BMI)
A Division of Lyons Partnership, L.P.
All Rights Reserved   Used by Permission

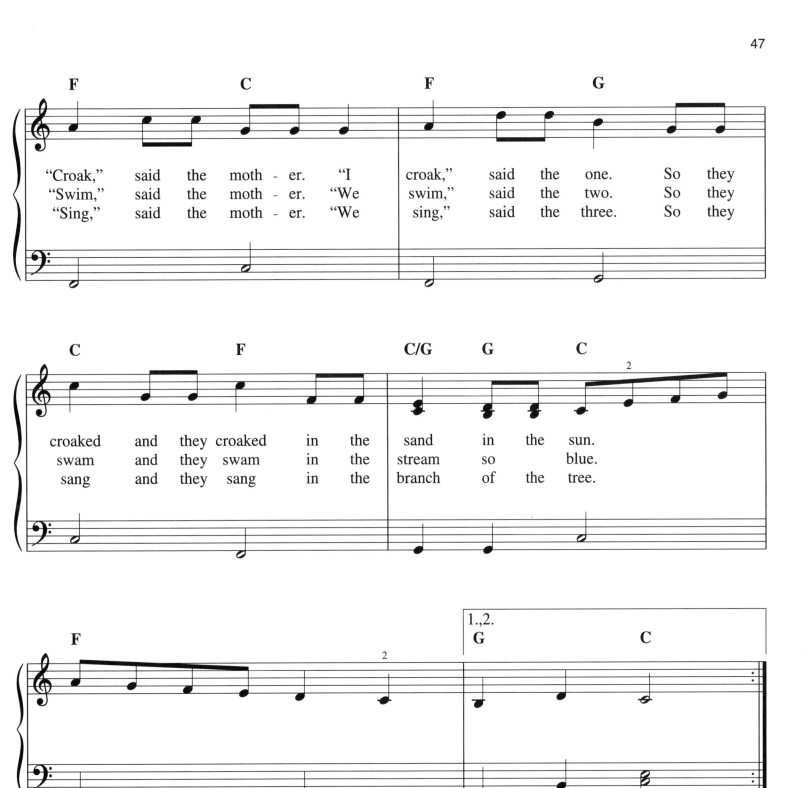

"Croak," said the moth - er. "I croak," said the one. So they
"Swim," said the moth - er. "We swim," said the two. So they
"Sing," said the moth - er. "We sing," said the three. So they

croaked and they croaked in the sand in the sun.
swam and they swam in the stream so blue.
sang and they sang in the branch of the tree.

rit.

PEOPLE HELPING OTHER PEOPLE

Music and Lyrics by
PHILIP A. PARKER

Moderately fast

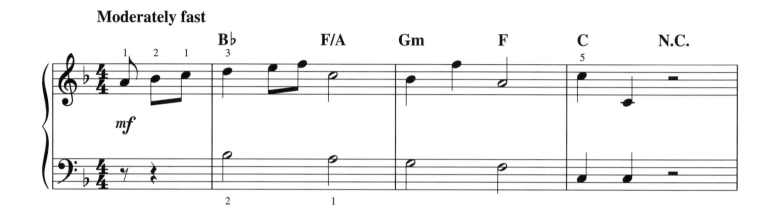

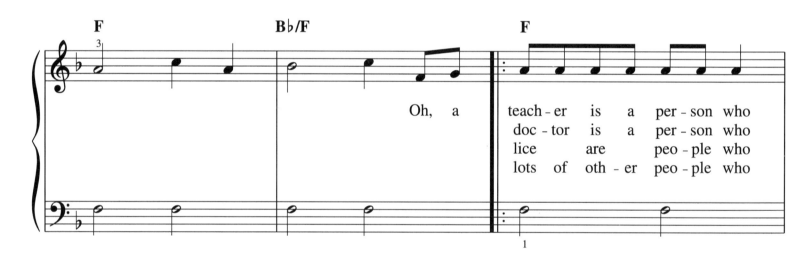

Oh, a

teach - er is a per - son who
doc - tor is a per - son who
lice are peo - ple who
lots of oth - er peo - ple who

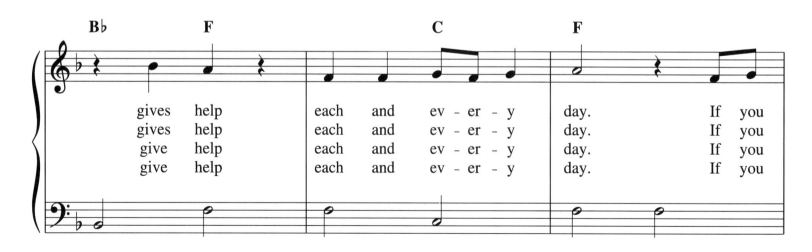

gives help each and ev - er - y day. If you
gives help each and ev - er - y day. If you
give help each and ev - er - y day. If you
give help each and ev - er - y day. If you

Copyright © 1992 Shimbaree Music (ASCAP)
A Division of Lyons Partnership, L.P.
All Rights Reserved   Used by Permission

50

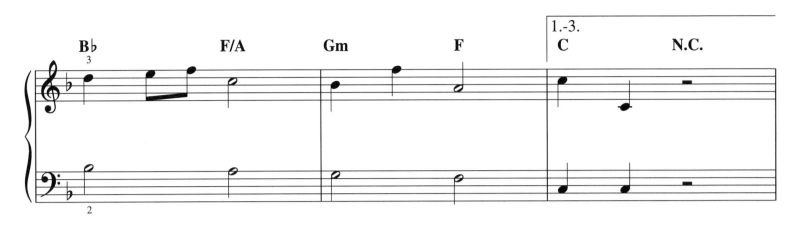

Oh,   a
The po -
There   are

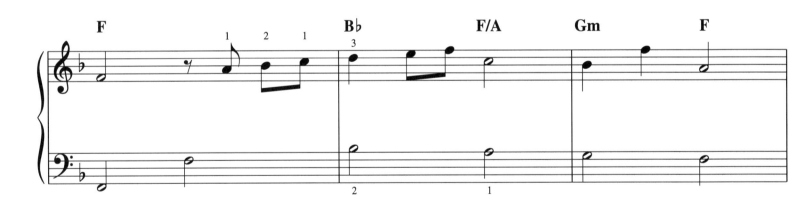

THE SISTER SONG

Music and Lyrics by
PHILIP A. PARKER

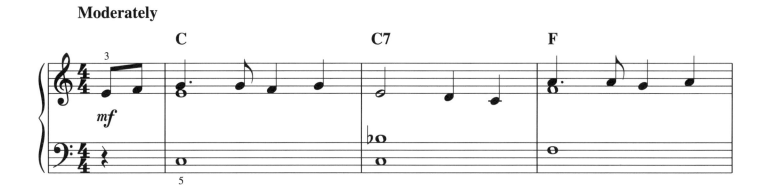

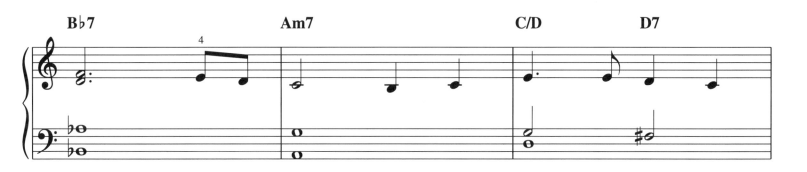

Some - times we're | real close
great big

friends. | We stay up late and talk at night. Oth - er times we
hug | when __ she was feel - ing bad. And ___ then a - gain I've

Copyright © 1992 Shimbaree Music (ASCAP)
A Division of Lyons Partnership, L.P.
All Rights Reserved   Used by Permission

52

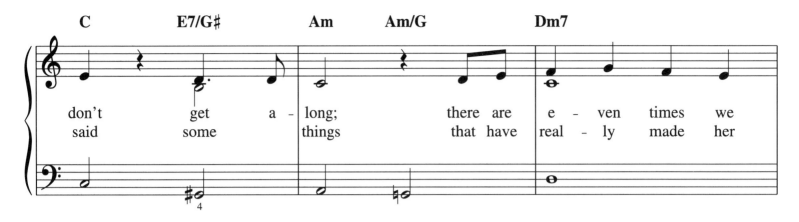

don't get a - long; there are e - ven times we
said some things that have real - ly made her

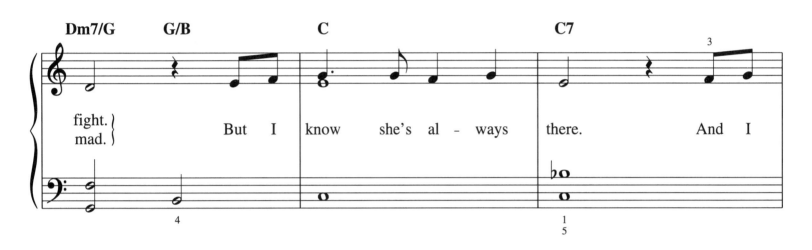

fight. } But I know she's al - ways there. And I
mad. }

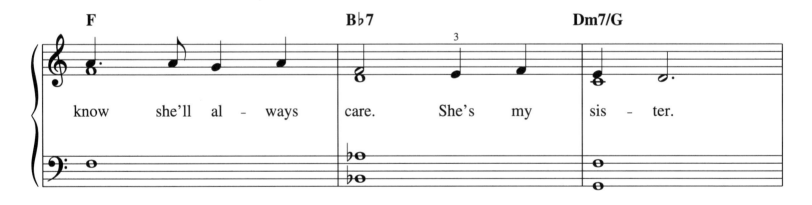

know she'll al - ways care. She's my sis - ter.

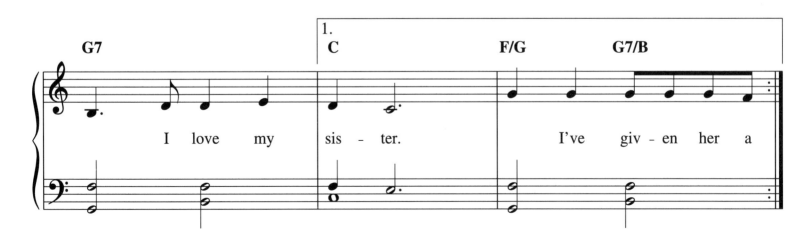

I love my sis - ter. I've giv - en her a

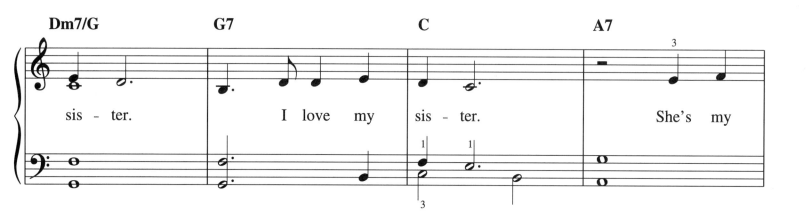

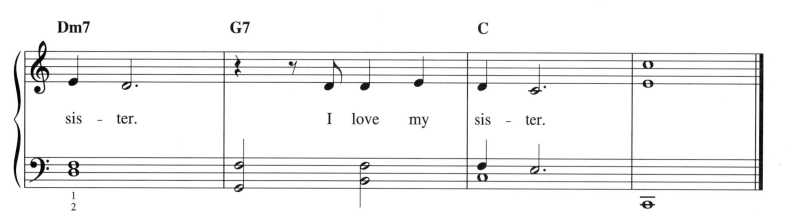

SOMEONE TO LOVE YOU FOREVER

Music and Lyrics by STEPHEN BATES BALTES
and LORY LAZARUS

Moderately

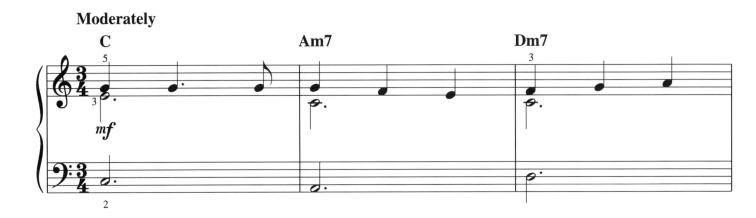

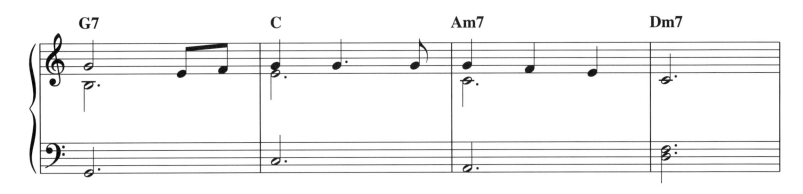

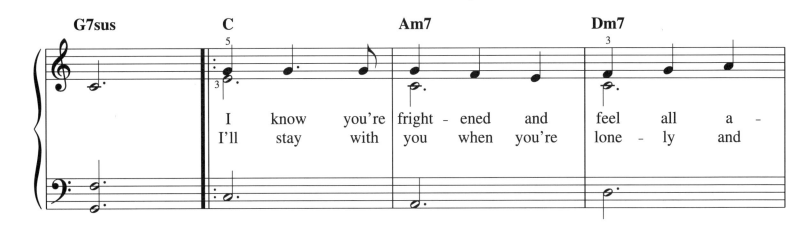

I know you're fright - ened and feel all a -
I'll stay you're with you when you're lone - ly and

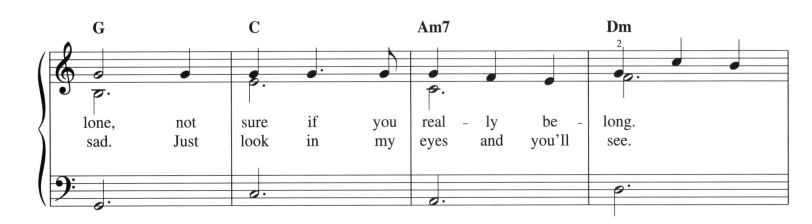

lone, not sure if you real - ly be - long.
sad. Just look in my eyes and you'll see.

Copyright © 1995 Shimbaree Music (ASCAP)
A Division of Lyons Partnership, L.P.
All Rights Reserved   Used by Permission

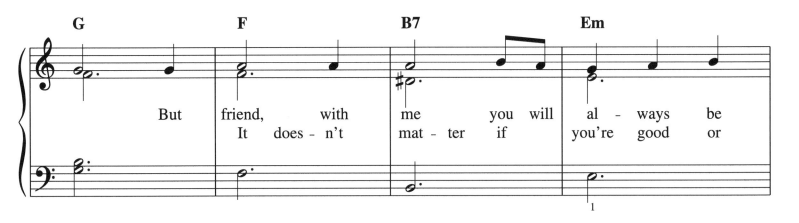

But friend, with me you will al - ways be
It does - n't mat - ter if you're good or

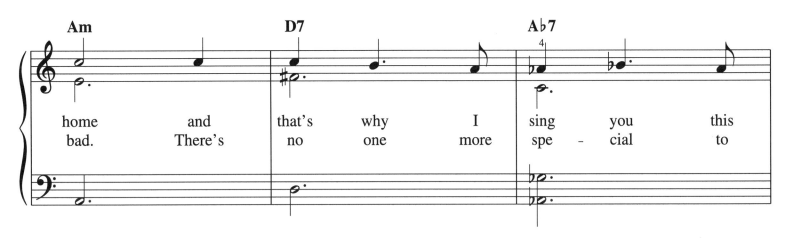

home and that's why I sing you this
bad. And There's no one more spe - cial to

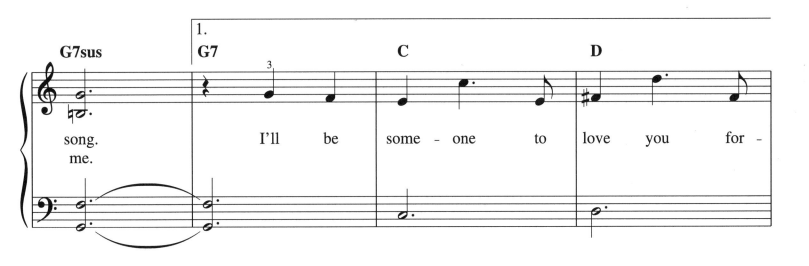

song. I'll be some - one to love you for -
me.

ev - er.

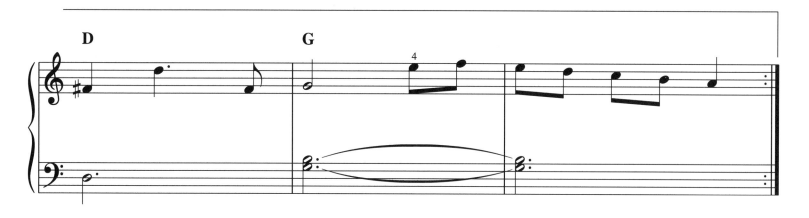

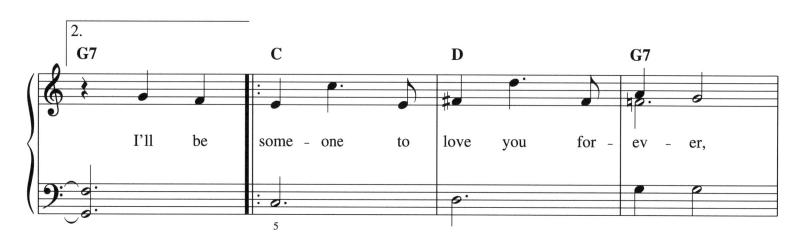

I'll be some - one to love you for - ev - er,

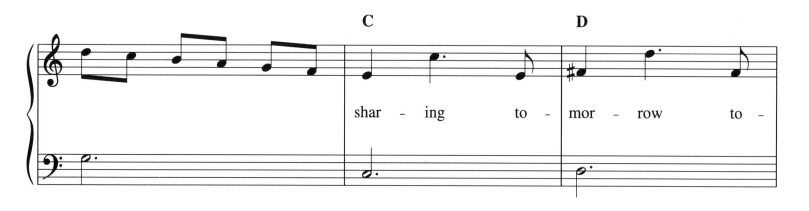

shar - ing to - mor - row to -

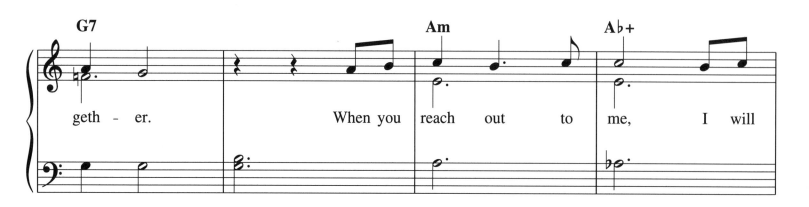

geth - er. When you reach out to me, I will

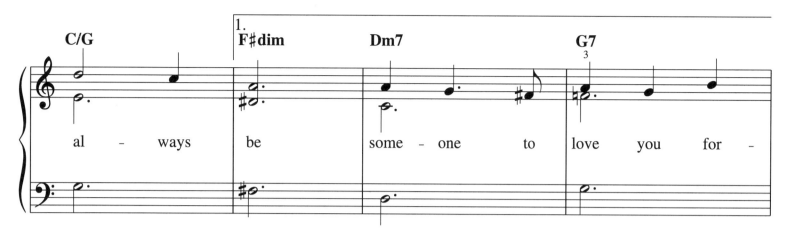

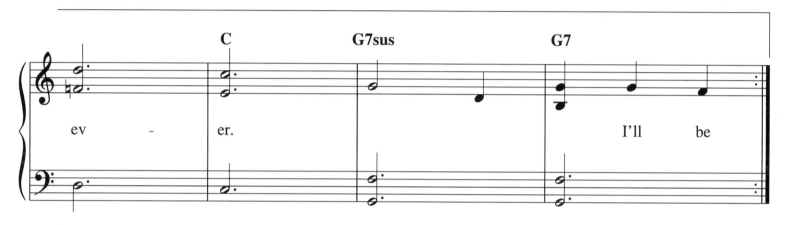

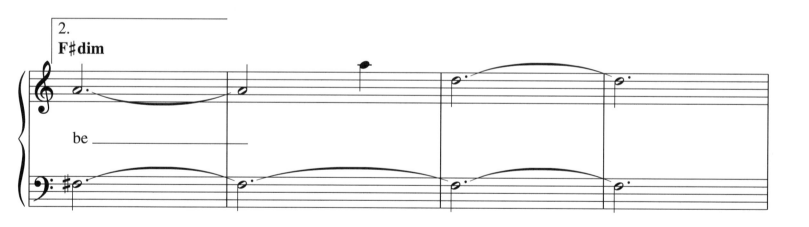

TAKING TURNS

Music and Lyrics by
PHILIP A. PARKER

Copyright © 1992 Shimbaree Music (ASCAP)
A Division of Lyons Partnership, L.P.
All Rights Reserved   Used by Permission

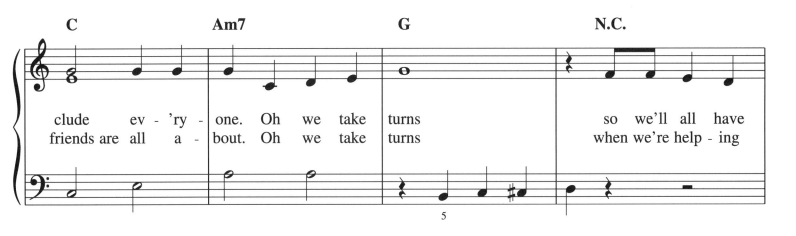

clude   ev - 'ry - one.   Oh   we   take   turns   so   we'll   all   have
friends   are   all   a - bout.   Oh   we   take   turns   when   we're   help - ing

fun.

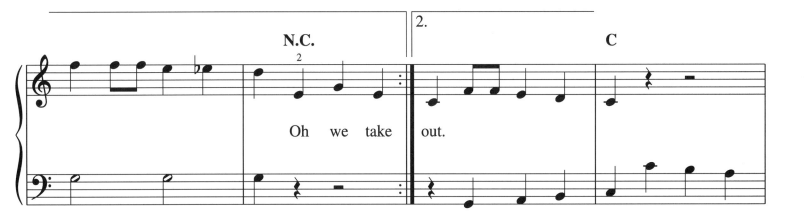

Oh   we   take   out.

THERE ARE SEVEN DAYS IN A WEEK

Traditional Music ("Clementine")
Lyrics by LAWRENCE I. HARON

Cheerfully, with a swing feel

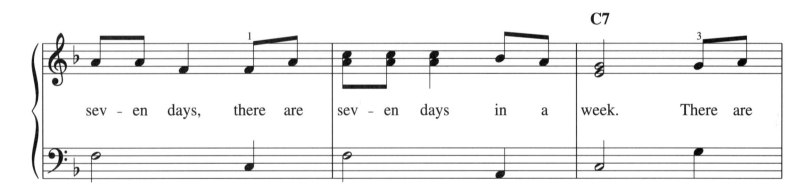

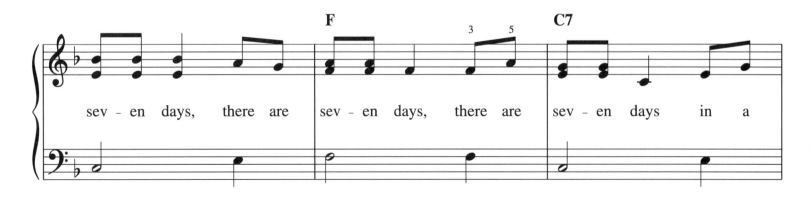

Lyrics and Arrangement Copyright © 1990 Shimbarah Music (BMI)
All Rights Reserved   Used by Permission

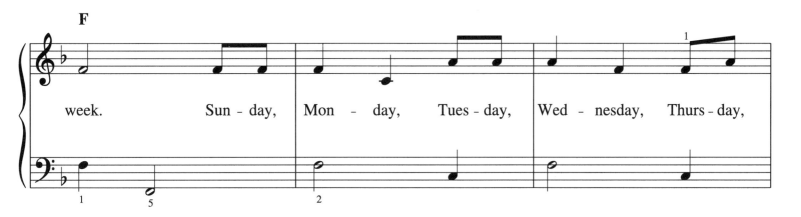

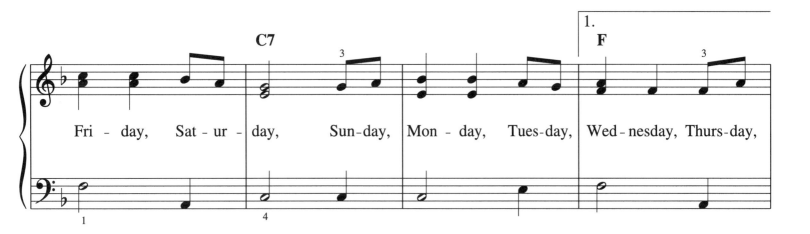

THE YUM-YUM SONG

Music and Lyrics by
ANGELO NATALIE

Copyright © 1997 Shimbaree Music (ASCAP)
All Rights Reserved   Used by Permission

YOU CAN COUNT ON ME

Music and Lyrics by
ANGELO NATALIE

Copyright © 1997 Shimbaree Music (ASCAP)
All Rights Reserved   Used by Permission

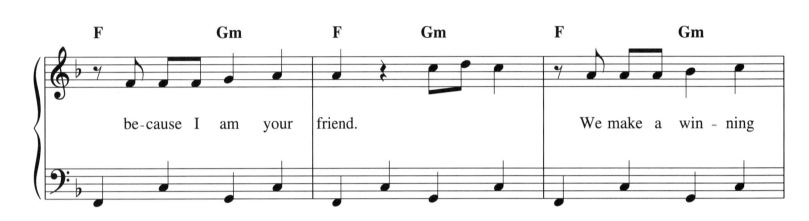

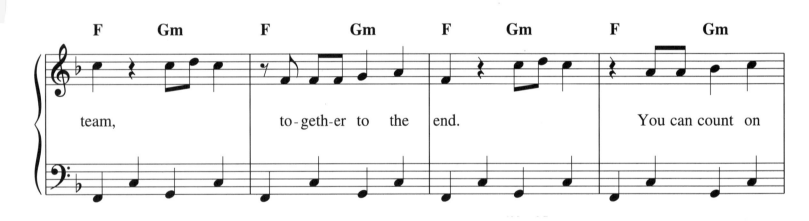

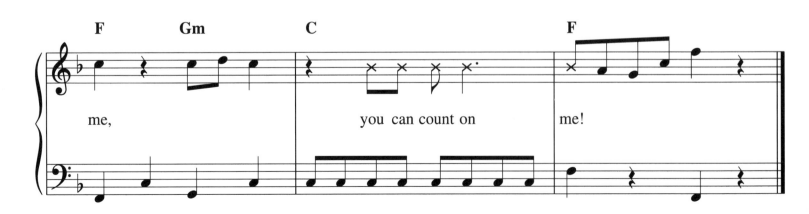

I LOVE YOU

Traditional Music ("This Old Man")
Lyrics by LEE BERNSTEIN

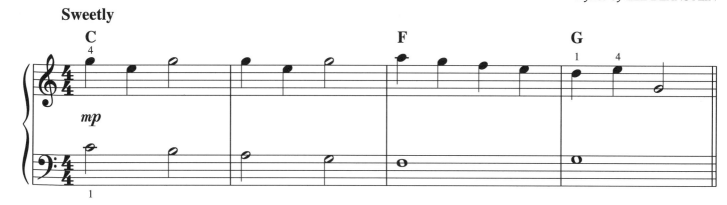

I love you, you love me; { we're a hap-py we're best friends like | fam-i-ly. friends should be. } With a

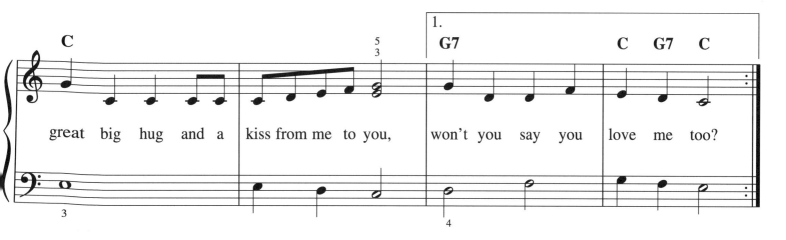

great big hug and a kiss from me to you, won't you say you love me too?

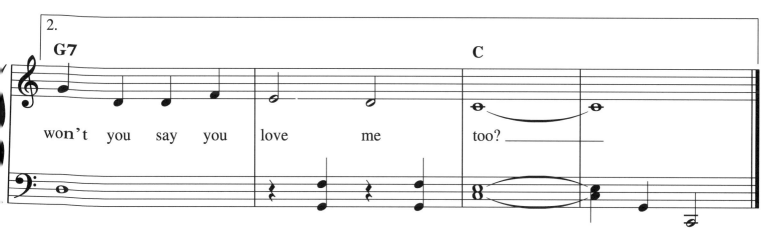

won't you say you love me too? _____

Copyright © 1983 Shimbarah Music (BMI)
A Division of Lyons Partnership, L.P.
All Rights Reserved   Used by Permission